Rhymes of Reflection

MATT BALANE

rhymes of reflection

matt balane

ISBN PRINT: **979-8-218-98933-0**

ISBN EBOOK: **979-8-218-98934-7**

COVER DESIGN & PHOTOGRAPHY: Fariss Ryan

thevirtualneighborhood.com

Illustrations: Images created with the assistance of DALL·E 2

intro poem

Rhymes of Reflection

This poetry book is cut into five sections

Identity, Nature, Connection,

Spoken Seeds and Introspection

A chance to do a personal inspection

An opportunity to encounter yourself

To take stock of your own mental health

To discover a deep trove of wealth

Into the depths of our hearts we delve

Thank you for joining on this trip to find

Treasures hidden inside my mind

Expressed through poetry, rhythm, & rhyme

Like emotional surgery, I open my heart

And allow the readers to rip it apart

Hoping that waves of healing impart

Life into your spirit like colors of art

Time for connection

Time for introspection

Lines of expression

Rhymes of reflection

identity

· · ·

Mother Islands

Caught inside the tension

Of different identities

Opposite reflections

Of two separate entities

Full blooded Filipino

First generation American

The states is all we know

But I don't have fairer skin

Disconnected from the islands

Bound to the states

Feel like a hybrid

It's hard to relate

When I don't speak

My native tongue

Always felt unique

Since I was young

Not Asian enough

Was what they thought

Insecurity struck

Affecting me a lot

. . .

Though I don't understand

The language of my folks

I still eat with my hands

With rice in my bowl

Tilapia, pancit

Nilaga, adobo

Calamansi, patis

Ube, and champorado

Burgers, BBQ

Hot dogs, steak

Meat loaf, beef stew

And Costco chicken bakes

My family really hustled

Great work ethics

Taught us how to struggle

It's in my genetics

Now they have expectations

Of our continued success

Cause they set the foundation

So I can build and be blessed

I've yet to see the Motherland

As I've been residing in the West

Babysat by Uncle Sam

Doesn't make me any less

My culture is adequate

This pride shines

No one can devalue it

This experience is mine

More

Society deems my worth

By how much I work

By career and job

By productive or not

But I am more than

The labor of my hands

Time cards and clock ins

Or professional whims

I am worthy because

I continue to get up

Despite the let downs

Frowns and grey clouds

My value remains steady because

I am becoming who I want to become

Despite my glaring flaws

Insecurities and scars

The fact that I am alive

Is honorable and prized

Cause life tried to end me

But blessings kept sending

. . .

If you judge based on performance

Know that life's work is enormous

So please pay me my dues

For it's a full-time job living in these shoes
12

Warrior

In the ring, time slows down.

A fight for glory, who will take the crown?

Every punch is a test of will,

Precise movements of sharpened skill.

A warrior's heart, with fists of thunder

When pressure rises who will fall under?

Blood, sweat, and tears inevitably shed,

Blocking all the shots aimed at my head.

Bobbing and weaving around like a dance,

Waiting patiently for a momentous chance.

To counter punch and regain control–

As this battle starts to finally take a toll.

Switch hitting as I change my stance,

Every inch is a distance I wish to advance.

A moment of peace as I hear the bell.

But more rounds to go fighting through hell.

Despite the challenge my mind is clear,

I press on forward and swallow fear.

I hear my coach's voice blaring loud–

Beyond the harsh roar of the crowd.

. . .

Win or lose I won't be phased.

I feel joy and pride as my hand is raised.

Through this quarrel I stand victorious–

Straight back to training 'cause I'm a warrior.

14

Fly

Out of the shadows

For once I am seen

Stuck in a battle

But somehow I'm free

Frozen in fear

Alone in a closet

Emotions feel weird

Now that I am honest

I have always dreamed

Of being at peace

With a voice that could sing

And beautiful black wings

Wearing feathers of lace

And joy blushing my face

In a foundation of grace

This high is healing my pain

Stalking the clouds

I strut to the sky

With hope as a gown

Love lining my eyes

I shadow my frowns

For now I can fly

Second Dawn

When I'm alone and feel the strain,

Hope lifts me like a dove through rain.

God's love, an endless helping hand,

Rebuilds my life from ash and sand.

Though words fall short of thanks to say,

I strive to show love, the Divine way.

Imperfect, yet She sees us all,

Equal, great or small.

Spirituality is more than name—it's life,

Overflowing joy, leaving behind strife.

I dropped the hate, began anew,

Shame gone, a clearer view.

I feel we're nearing the second dawn,

With greed and wickedness dragging us on.

Love of money blinds and speeds the end,

But faith and love will transcend.

26

Another year survived

Another battle won

Amidst the darkest fights

I live to see the sun

Cheers to 26

A miraculous feat

Peace to those lost

Adrift in afterlife's stream

Thankful for friendship

Fatherhood and family

Priceless gifts

An anchor for my sanity

I'm finally finding hope

Beginning to feel free

Starting to seek my goals

Re-finding the strength to dream

28

28 rotations around the sun

28 years since life begun

Since then I have loved and lost

Time has made me pay the cost

Bravely getting up every day

Harshly fighting along the way

I've learned that every breath

Is a reminder that I am blessed

As souls come and go

Along life streams flow

We remember those at peace

Resting in eternal sleep

How we miss our beloved

Their presence we so covet

To spend another moment close

And know they're not alone

We hope heaven is kind

With peace for all to find

For earth can often be hell

As problems commonly dwell

. . .

Fatherhood motivates

Friendship cultivates

Blessings amidst

With depth and width

I've conquered another year

For that, we shout and cheer

Wonder and adventure await

As I wander into year 28

Best of Both Worlds

Rigid definitions

Confined positions

Severely masculine

Extremely feminine

Boxers or panties

Tight clothes or baggy

Bold and manly

Girly and sassy

Those roles are a noose

To reality and truth

For me to let loose

I cannot choose

Fitting a mold

Is selling my soul

To do what I'm told

Is being controlled

All boy or all girl

I can't pick a role

The best of both worlds

Is what I behold

Enough

Fear

Insecurity

Imperfection

All the while,

I am enough

Adequate

Despite flaws

Valuable

Despite doubts

I am enough

Worthy

In light of failure

Mess ups

And mishaps

I am enough

I Am Them

You speak harsh words

Against her

Against him

Attacking a thing

You don't understand

Blaming a person

Who you don't know

In these strikes

Among these rumors

You attack me

For I am her

For I am him

I am them too

connection

. . .

Sweet Red

Your color is passion

A scarlet attraction

Sense of refreshment

Smooth as velvet

Your power is potent

Aroma flows when opened

A smell so seductive

Lustfully voluptuous

Your taste is sweet

A delectable treat

Calming my cravings

A drink so amazing

Your love intoxicates

Like wine of old age

Poured into my glass

Heart filled fast

You are my sweet red

I'm a drunken mess

Stumbling around

In your love I drown

Little Rose

I remember when I first held you

Tiny hands and feet

Little head of hair

With huge eyes that peered

Into the depths of my soul

In one glance

In one instant

I was marked

With an eternal love

An unbreakable bond

Which tied us forever

My little rose

How I've watched you bloom

Into a whole garden

Of color and vibrancy

Oh how I've seen you blossom

Into more than we ever imagined

From a single sprout

To my entire world

Your beautiful petals fall

To reveal brighter ones

In the wake of your growth

You grow me

You teach me to be

More than I ever thought

More than I ever imagined

Your roots have entangled

My entire soul

With nourishment and purpose

I love you more than flowers

More than words could express

More than actions could demonstrate

More than emotions could feel

I love you, my Leila Rose

May your roots go deeper

May your seeds sprout farther

May your thorns grow sharper

May your petals get bigger

May you be more than I ever was

Jessica

Once a girl full of hopes and bright dreams,

Free to wander and imagine wild scenes.

But life dealt her a blow, her spirit dimmed deep,

Now she's a lovely caged bird that can't sing.

Wings once open, now broken, can't soar,

Silent beak sealed tight, she dreams no more.

Disappointments piled up, hope grew thin,

So numb from the pain, she let darkness win.

Drugs dull her senses, she can't quit the strain,

Alcohol floods in, to wash away pain.

Her closest companion is Hennessy's burn,

Her heart stays shattered, with no love to return.

Her fiercest foe now her own troubled mind,

A battle within she can't leave behind.

But Jessica's story didn't end in despair,

She found a spark of hope lingering in the air.

A hand reached out from the shadows of doubt,

A friend, a community, helped pull her out.

She faced the mirror, saw beauty inside,

Embraced her flaws, rediscovered her pride.

Her wings began healing, she started to sing,

Freeing herself from addiction's cruel sting.

Self-love bloomed where the darkness had been,

She found peace in the strength growing within.

Now Jessica's soaring, no cage, no chains,

Her heart beats steady, no more heavy shame.

With a tribe around her, she learned how to rise,

The girl with dreams is now oh so alive.

Pretty Stranger

Times stops as we cross paths,

Blue glow– a single glance,

And I'm captivated,

While my mind is racing,

I wonder where you're from,

And who you will become,

I wonder who you are,

Your eyes as bright as stars,

One twinkle in the gloom,

And I'm swept away from you,

Because time moves too fast,

As this moment moves past,

A fork in the cosmic road,

To the heavens we go,

I do not know your name,

Yet it is okay,

For unto me you are

A pretty stranger

Still She Grows

A flower among the valley

Blooming as time unfolds

Planted in cities and alleys

Where innocence is unknown

Yet she grew

Seeds in a garden divided

But roots so deeply fixed

Living water she abides in

So this flower will live

Still see she grows

Other plants have died in dry grounds

Without others to help

But she has felt life where death surrounds

Around her others fell

Yet she grew

But I am not a gardener

Merely an observer

Who has seen a flower

That has a heart so pure

And still she grows

Touch

Your touch can speak

What words fail to express

You embrace me

With loving sounds unheard

I hear your heart

Through our silent contact

And feel your love

Inside quiet moments

We can make songs

Without a melody

Just our bodies

Expressing the music

So let's listen deep

As we sing together

Here

In the cold breeze

As the wind screams

In the white snow

As the ice glows

You are here

In the grey clouds

As I fly around

In the new city

Hiking stiff peaks

You are with me

In the coffee cup

When aroma erupts

In the chilled brew

When I sip through

You are here

In joyous laughter

When memories capture

In heart-to-heart talks

When many paths cross

You are with me

Zapped

Mind and heart captured

As prisoners of hope

Reaching for it's guard

In fear of losing this feeling of

Ecstasy and belonging

A smile took me in

Lost in her eyes

Validated by her story

And appreciated by her touch

Refreshed under her voice

Enchanted by her words

Zapped by this connection

A.C.

Any time I see you

Nerves go away

Negative feelings fade

Intertwined hearts

Eternity is ours

Captivated by your gaze

Every moment is magical

Nothing compares to you

Devotion deep and true

Always trustworthy

Naturally beautiful

As we fan love's flame

Freeze

I can picture it now

Snow falling in the background

Wind caressing my head

Water resting on my legs

Cold presenting itself

But my heart is warm

Those eyes are sparkling

Your nose is freezing

Lips are shivering

Teeth are chattering

Our kisses freeze in time

For a moment

Nothing else exists

Let me remember this

nature

. . .

When I Die

When I die

Scatter me among the waves

Send my ashes to a safe place

Give me the freedom I never had

Endless searching

Constant waiting

For impossible solace

When I die

Place me upon a mountain

Lay my remains high above

To fly like I always wanted

Cause I've been low

Beneath my potential

Sinking into oblivion

When I die

Sew me into a garden

Rest my remnants in a fruitful land

To live amongst nature

United with Mother Earth

As I'm disconnected from life

Awaiting rebirth

Constellations

With my head tilted up, it fascinates my mind

How all countries of the world share only one sky

With a shine so bright illuminating eyes

From a higher elevation where birds can't fly

Always present, but invisible by day

It leads my mind into disarray

When light fades and darkness stays

The stars reveal a celestial maze

Helping pirates in navigation

Or simply a visual fascination

Always watching over every generation

I stare into eyes of great constellations

Holding onto questions tight and dear

Being so near, but origin's unclear

Connecting the dots as darkness appears

Yearning for answers I sit and peer

Nature's Song

I came here

To hear nature sing

But only windy whispers,

Rustling leaves,

And chirps sound.

An ear met with quiet.

Being here I realize,

Silence is the song

My soul needed to hear.

Rushing Water

Forgiveness flows as rushing water

From the heart of loving Father

Cuts & scrapes, hurts & wounds

Cleansed & healed, life anew

Pools of grace connect

Bridging gaps of heart & head

Wash my streams of thought

with truths my soul forgot

Like rocks fade to sand

Break down my broken plans

Remove the silhouette

and show me who I am

How quickly I forget

When panic steals my breath

This life, it ebbs & flows

and crashes at the end

So now I bask in beauty

and hold tomorrow loosely

Watching guilt drift farther

I drown in rushing water

Wind

The wind moves free without a care,

Through open fields and skies laid bare,

It whispers secrets none can hear,

Yet howls loudly far and near.

It dances through the autumn trees,

A gentle sigh, a restless breeze,

It lifts the leaves in swirling flight,

And sends them soaring into night.

It has no path, it has no bound,

Yet everywhere its touch is found.

A nomad, wild, yet calm within,

The ever-changing breath of wind.

It plays with clouds and bends the sea,

A silent song, forever free,

Unseen, untamed, it drifts and roams,

A wanderer that calls no home.

Summer

A sunny day in June

The warm breeze looms

Joyful sounds and tunes

Repel moods of gloom

A hot evening in July

Sunburns from sunshine

Nature always replies

With light and blue skies

An airy night in August

The heat is at it's calmest

Past two months were the hottest

Flashes of change as comets

Whispers

Nature whispers quietly

My heart responds silently

Wind controls the band

Trees, leaves, and plants

They sway, play, and dance

To Mother Nature's chants

Rocks provide the rhythm

Bugs jive along with 'em

Animals know the system

Humans should watch and listen

Through day-time and summer

Dark nights and winter

Songs are delivered

Nature, she whispers

Sea

Lost at sea

Tempest breeze

Raging winds

All I see

Aquatic maze

Destructive waves

Chaotic spins

A heart untamed

Freezing cold

Powerful hold

Abandoned ships

Bitter soul

Towering thoughts

Oceanic rot

Misguided trip

Deathly plot

Nature evolves

Plans dissolve

Sorrowful mist

Life unresolved

Storms

Nature is both beauty and beast

Wonderful sights to behold from west to east

Yet ravenous as a monster out to feast

Leaving behind a trail of destruction and deceased

Storms unfurling like a creature from the deep

Ripping through the sky's fragile seam

With tough claws that are sharp and extreme

Rivers bow down and offer their streams

Lightning strikes with teeth, jagged and vile

Its voice a growl, thunderous and wild

No empathy towards man, woman, or child

Entire cities and states defiled

Mountains tremble beneath its roar

As heaven's punishment pours

Trees bow down and kiss the floor

While houses and cars are flooded to the core

Rain sweeps away our human vanity

As hurricanes swirl into insanity

Distorting communities and families

Exposing our powerless humanity

Ocean

The ocean is mysterious and vast

Secrets drowning away the past

Preserving riddles in its depths

Safe from human threats

In pitch blackness far from shallow

Creatures lie in dark shadows

Where light is sucked into a vacuum

And the cold is eerie like a ghost passed you

Strange gigantic creatures

With bioluminescent features

At the bottom of the ocean lies mysteries

Broken down remains of human history

Kept below in Poseidon's chest

Locked away with great success

Oceanic depths parallel outer space

Putting human smallness in place

All there is to do is marvel and wonder

About infinite treasures which lie down under

introspection

. . .

Creative

As I wipe the dust off my notepad—

A callused heart turns fragile,

A closed mind opens.

With eyes shut I see possibilities

Of creation & destruction,

Of assurance & reluctance,

Of beautiful & ugly.

With this pen

I travel lands undiscovered—

Standing on peaks of victory

And marching through dark valleys of defeat.

With these words

I express the inexpressible,

Explain the unexplainable,

And imagine that which is not.

The powers of life & death literally at my fingertips.

Muse surges within my spirit—

I can feel the rumbling.

Shaking my rib cages til heart flutters freely,

Punching my gut til stanzas manifest

From the depths of my soul.

Now this,

This my beloved,

Is what it's like to be a creative.

Uncertainty

Today's absolute

Could be tomorrow's memory

The solidity of truth

Shaken by time's energy

Fading foundations

We walk upon

Inevitable changes

Despite our wants

Hope

Disappointment setting in.

The sense of letdown

After great expectations.

Pain upon my soul,

But hope refuses to fade.

Hope sees beyond "now" into "what could be"-

Believing "it is possible"

Yet prepared for lack of execution

And unfulfilled imagination.

Hope gives more than insight,

Providing strength to endure hardships.

When the hopeful

Surrounded on all sides,

Fights against the odds,

Hope empowers the impossible.

Hope is risky.

It is of the most vulnerable.

Which is why hope is beautiful.

That is why it brings healing.

That is why hope creates intimacy,

Because in order to love,

One must hope first.

Analysis Paralysis

Over analysis

Leads to paralysis

Indecisiveness

Can't decide for shit

Too many options

Feels so exhausting

Crippling anxiety

Lacking propriety

Fear of wrong choice

Fear of using voice

Fear of missing out

Fear and heavy doubt

I need to learn

When it's my turn

It's okay to commit

My answers are legit

Trust yourself

You don't need help

You just need assurance

This is a natural occurrence

Drowning

She drinks from the bottle

To wash down the sorrow

Til a full heart turns hollow

Saying, "I'll do better tomorrow"

She drowns out all her fears

He restrains with handcuffs

Pointing fingers and loaded guns

Yelling until rage overcomes

Tasing another— his heart goes numb

He drowns out all his fears

She neglects her own health

Works to serve someone else

Acquiring money and wealth

To compensate for a poor sense of self

She drowns out all her fears

He watches pornography

Like virtual sodomy

To feel "power" and "autonomy"

Because an inner animosity

He drowns out all his fears

• • •

We hide our value

Believing the untrue

On our hearts like a tattoo

We feel that we have to

Drown out all our fears

Jump

Should I jump in or not?

Adventure lies on the other side

Should I go now or stop?

There's beauty in the pursuit of life

Afraid yet excited

Unsure outcomes of risk and reward

Traveling unguided

Almost feel what I'm moving towards

My heart says I should jump

My conscience declares the opposite

The divide makes me stumped

Such decisions create inconfidence

Fear mirroring past scenes

When brave risk turned into tragedy

With one glimpse of love seen

Distance disappeared dramatically

So I dove into abyss

Hoping for shining lights to save me

Searching for a pure kiss

Knowing it would lead me to safety

• • •

This time might be greater

Thus fulfilling these utter longings

If I step beyond "safer"

Into danger to find belonging

The heart cannot be stopped

Adventure lies on the other side

I will go unstopped

There's beauty in the pursuit of life

Labyrinth of Thoughts

Deep secrets lie in the corridors of the mind

Winding like a maze, truths we seek to find

We wander endlessly in this labyrinth,

Lost and adrift in streams of consciousness,

The paths are narrow and rarely straight

Bends, turns, and dead ends await

A silent echo, faint yet clear

Of hopes, doubts, love, and fear

As we press on, through shadowed halls

Where distant voices rise and fall

We search for answers hidden from sight

Within the darkness, flickers light

Despite it being easy to get lost

The reward is worth the risk and the cost

For in introspection we gain

A spark of muse like a gentle flame

For though our senses may seem blind

There's wisdom woven in the mind

And every twist and turn reveals

A part of us that slowly heals

Power Outage

When everything is quiet

Technology is silent

No tablets playing

No TVs relaying

No fish tanks humming

No fridges running

Nothing cooking

Boredom pushing

Yet it's calming

Simply soothing

The slowing of hours

We're out of power

My Escape

My mind goes numb

My soul wastes away

My heart shuts down

With the sound of a beep

One simple click

To forget my worries

To escape reality

To calm my heart

Just a touch

A slight vibration

Quick stimulation

Vivid animation

Mindless scrolling

Never ending search

Imaginative muse

A vague illusion

Television screens

Video games

Musical melodies

And iPhones

Beautiful Gems

Beautiful gems

So bright and colorful

They could make any clothing look rich

Seemingly too nice to even hold

It's as though they should be put on display

Protected from unclean hands

How could their value ever be determined?

Such an impossible task

To simply try to calculate

For our minds are too limited

No price tag would do them justice

Yet they are sold by blind merchants

At too low of a cost

They make profit selling precious stones

Because the gems were not earned

They were priceless gifts taken by force

What a shame it is

They're not taken care of

Evil hands hold them

Creating a lackluster appearance

But it's just an illusion

For gems are so beautiful

spoken seeds

. . .

Drugs

Everybody can tell that I've been different lately. Friends look into my eyes and see something new. Family noticing the change too. And it can all be traced back to when I did those things I said I'd never do-- again. Room-mates are aware of the distortion in my facial expressions. Knowing I've been using medication to cope with depression. Now there's substance in my system. Forsaking known wisdom. Betraying my sworn intentions and lessons I learned before that told me don't use it anymore. Big homie told me to try it, so I did once. But one led to two, two led to eight. It all adds up. Now it's something I crave more than lunch in the middle of the day when I still haven't ate. I need this. Without it I'm anxious. Enraged and impatient. Pacing the pavement afraid when I can't taste it. Amazing how I even stopped back then cause I don't feel like Matt without it. It gives me strength to believe, courage to achieve, and honesty to process my history of misery from 2017.

Listen when I say I am an abuser. I've used marijuana, cigarettes, and vodka. Kratom, Norcos, and Narcotics. Edibles, sleeping pills, and THC products. Pain killers, codeine, and shrooms. Spice, salvia, and dabs. Cocaine, hash, and wax. When I say I've done the max these are facts. This liver is probably crying to be delivered. Got all these addictions from afflictions but this one seems different. Without this I feel emotionless, brokenness over-flowing. Tolerance growing I've been raising dosages. Going through the motions. I've been doping my soul with hope.

Hope deferred makes the heart sick. So hope internalized within gives lift when I twitch and itch for a fix. Instead of twisting and lighting a spliff. Or crushing and snorting a brick. This substance is available through 2 twigs and a crucifix. Crucifying hopelessness and resurrecting with this drug. I threw it away when the times got rough but now my heart can't get enough. On it my heart feels stronger. Honestly hope was forgotten. Said I wouldn't bother. Because last time I did the road got harder, night times longer, my mind much darker, farther from God, my hope was slaughtered. Suicide talking, past sins haunting, depression was sovereign. I still got hella problems but they're not the author of my book. Hope in

God is. Now I'm ready to conquer. It's letting me heal. It fuels my will. It tells me to stay still when I feel emotionally ill.

I still battle depression, rejection, disconnection, and pressure but this time I'm obsessed with a new drug named hope. So this is for my addicts. Caught up in habits, living in havoc, as tragic accidents continue to happen. Losing your passion asking thousands of questions but hearing no answer. God sees you. God knows you. God is with you.

———

Mend

Intro:

Heart beats increase. The creases around their mouths peak into smiles. While butterflies beat against their rib cages. Gazes lost into one another. Raptured in the ecstasy of wonder and adventure. They've been traveling for weeks. In love. Exploring this journey in the confines of time. Their hearts intertwined. Diving into the mystery of romance.

Time to embrace:

Comfort. Security. Joy. In this season flowers of connection bloom. Nature bears beautiful fruits of embrace and their roots take place. Vivid colors on the surface. Life birthing underneath.

Life emerging from the deep depths within.

In the grounds of this relationship their love can live. Trust shines like the sunlight. Two seeds side by side growing in an opportune time.

Time to tear:

Doubt in the eyes. A smile on the face but torn on the inside. There's conflict. And what was once united is now divided and no matter how hard he tries to deny it, he can't hide it. They were high flying above now love looks like it's dying. Seconds turn to minutes and minutes turn to hours. Sweet turning to sour. Cause this tearing apart has been growing for days and they can't ignore it's power. They refuse to let go. They choose to still hold. But this hole in their soul is eroding their hope slowly.

Time to give up:

The heart is a muscle. This couple is troubled with atrophy. Those walls of the kingdom they built together, are torn down. All that's left is apathy. Their weary hands hold onto hopeless hope.

Calloused by the challenges of a broken soul. Pain out of control. Tears flooding the floor. And dreams crashing down like waves on the shore. They are exhausted. No days off this battle is constant. The insults and ill words are arrows. Shot at their partner's heart. Shot at their target. They both feel heartless. So regardless of their history. Their future fades quickly under the pressure of the present reality. They are giving up.

———

Grandpa Tribute Poem

Grandpa, you are a pioneer. You surfed over waves of fear to come here from the Philippines. Never letting issues interfere or problems come between your ambitions. Resting deep in the American Dream, maybe that's why you told me not to call you Lolo? Crossing the Pacific Ocean with focus and utmost devotion to your family. Establishing a lineage of men and women who stomp on mental illness and persevere through the hardest hardships.

See my grandpa is a gardener. Sowing seeds of legacy, bearing fruitfully just like your calamansi tree and your garden in our backyard. I could feel your very breath breathing through mine. Your voice echoing inside as I sing to the heavens.

You know, my grandpa is a comedian. Anointed with joy. Extracting laughs as he gasps for air between his own jokes with a cackle that sounds more like literal choking than actually laughing. My grandpa dares you to smile. Corny jokes like "You better learn how to cook pancit, not pan-shit!" As he cracks up and walks away rubbing his belly.

Grandpa is a provider. Upon his sacrifice and hard work our whole family tree is established. Long hours as a federal accountant to move your kids to the states.

Grandpa you are our rock. Solid, unshakable, courageous, and strong. When all is falling down, on your shoulder we lean on. Like Uncle Iroh, guiding a destructive Prince Zuko.

You are like glue. How you took the shattered fragments of our family and pieced them together like a beautiful mosaic. Single-handedly holding us together even after you're own son unalived himself in '05. So without you our family is nothing more than broken glass. Divided. Scattered. Lost.

Although I know my grandpa is gone I know he's never forgotten. Absent from this body but present with the Lord. My grandpa is united. I see him greeted at the gates by his mother, father, and beloved son Reggie.

I am a Balane. The world may take my time, my money, my efforts, my energy but never my last name. So I will walk worthy as such for the rest of my days. Knowing you're watching over us from a safer place. Grandpa we love you. Beyond you being a lover, fighter, and provider— You are, and always will be, my grandpa.

Finding Meaning Poem

My journey started on March 1, 2021 as I lost my wife, mother of my child, and my best friend Tiala to her battle with postpartum depression, PTSD, and other mental health issues. I've always thought that grief comes in stages. Move from 1, 2, 3, 4, then 5 on a step-by-step basis. But I learned that grief comes in phases, as we fade in, then out, then back into these different emotional spaces. I thought acceptance was the final destination. But it's actually an invitation to the last phase: finding meaning.

David Kessler coined this phrase describing how there's a way to remember who've we've lost with more love than pain. And I stand here today, to say, it's possible. I know trauma can rot your soul, leaving you lost and dull, like surviving another minute is the largest obstacle. I promise though, healing is available. I don't say this lightly, cause you might be: Hopelessly broken down, drowning in a thousand pounds of emotion, crying so many tears you could probably fill an ocean.

How all the happy moments with them turn into waves of regret. Wishing that I did more to love them harder. Wishing, I could've held them a little bit longer, as their presence is present in heaven but too far out of our human comprehension. It's okay to miss them. Your pain is just proof of your love for them. This pain you feel proves that your love is real. The cold emptiness is remembrance of how warm we felt in their company. I've spent so much time frustrated searching for a logical explanation til I had the revelation that there isn't one.

I embarked on a journey where there is no arrival. No matter how you paint it, no matter how you explain it, there's no amount of information that could heal a broken heart. I could wander into the wilderness of "what ifs" at any moment but I know I'll just get lost. So the only way for me to go is forward. Finding meaning gives me strength to move towards a life of healing. So now, the question is how?

For me, to find meaning is to choose life after suicide. To stare at the face of hopelessness and dare to dream for a beautiful future despite the devastation of my past. Finding meaning looks like keeping our hearts open although our trauma provokes us to become hard and calloused. Finding meaning looks like loving others the way our loved ones did while they were still here.

So with the strength of my grandpa by my side, and the memory of my wife and my uncle on my mind, I decide to find meaning in the legacy they left for me by caring for people and holding empathy. I'll choose life by raising Leila up high to the sky like Tiala did. I see her every time that I see my daughter so I will love Leila in her honor. All her life she longed for a home, so I will build community, fellowship, and a family worthy of her vision. Forever and always may she rest in peace.

 And as I write this years later, while I still feel the pain of loss, I find solace in the power it's brought. Because grief hasn't seemed to become smaller, my heart just manages to grow stronger. So for anyone struggling, I hope for your recovery. To everybody dealing with suicidal thoughts or ideations, please know your presence is valued here. Remember you're not alone though it feels like it. And It's okay to not be okay. I'm so sorry you're going through this. You are irreplaceable and special. Your story is important. So please reach out and let someone hear it. Express your stress because you are not a burden. I know after the trauma of the past it can be hard to see healing. So for anyone grieving, I hope this poem helps you find meaning.

———

Cheese

I have a love-hate relationship with cheese. There's nothing else that could pull on my heart strings like these. But it hurts me to my core when I eat it excessively. I am a mouse so my obsession is expected, but the irony is in how my body actually rejects it. When I roam the house, checking every crevasse, searching under the couch and hidden corners. My stomach jumps in anticipation. When I meet other mice, it's in the back of my mind with high expectations. The constant contemplation leaves me in agony waiting.

It's like my heart is Swiss and the pain is sharp as cheddar. Feeling the blues so blue cheese makes me feel better. I got a soft spot for Brie, so don't deny me my feta when I'm fed up. This cheese reminds me that I am me. Bringing me back to childhood memories. I smell the asiago. Wheels of parmigiano-reggiano in sight. Way before my vision became gruyere smoky and my attitude Roquefort salty. I binge mozzarella now to remind me that I'm a mouse. So I will maneuver through the house in search of Gouda. Although once it's over, it stinks like Gorgonzola and I want to throw up. At least I'm full. Eating so much I become dull. My desires can no longer take control when I give into it. I have an obsession and I acknowledge it. I am a mouse, I love cheese but I hate that I'm lactose intolerant.

————

My Job

People always ask what I do for work. But every time they did, I used to get insecure about my answer. So let me explain. In March 2020 I lost my job, like many others did, because of the COVID-19 pandemic. Thankfully, on April 14, right in the middle of the whole world shutting down I started a different job. One that still employs me today. Although it's a rough, tough, don't pay me enough job, it definitely has its benefits. It's crazy how I stumbled into this occupation 'cause my lack of qualifications. Like I was the complete opposite of every trait listed in the job description.

So I used to say it's something that wasn't for me. Rather rock a 9 to 5 or something less emotionally taxing or physically demanding cause this job costs you everything. Honestly, I got a degree in theology thinking I'd be in ministry. Wanted to be a pastor leading sheep to God's pastures. Helping others turn their lives to a new chapter.

After that phase in spiritual formation, I wanted to work in higher education. Walking students to their destination. Lastly, I dreamt about being a professional poet on the grandest stages while my music plays on radio stations. Instead I'm in a position I never really applied for. Imagine working somewhere that every time you get a promotion, you get less money, and more responsibility.

Picture a job where every quarter your duties change but you're still expected to perform at the same level of competency or higher. Imagine a workplace where you're on call 24/7 because you're the only one that could do what you do. My brothers and sisters, welcome to the lifestyle, day-in day-out, job of all jobs— Fatherhood, Motherhood, parenting.

I refer to this as a job not because it's a chore but just because it's hard work. Got promoted full time after my wife passed. I'm a father but not just a father. See when you're a girl-dad like me, you also have to be a singer and a dancer, belting out Disney songs and singing the latest Princess jams as your living room transforms into a stage.

When you're a parent you become chef. Cooking up chicken nuggies and spaghetti for the body while nurturing the mind with food for thought and encouragement for the soul. I'm not only a dad, I'm a construction worker, the way I build their confidence brick by brick, demolishing insecurities or anything that threatens to crack the foundation of their identity.

Being a dad means being a minister, because how we live our lives will be the first sermon they'll ever hear about God. We're also teachers because education starts in the home. Something like a judge, how we sentence our little ones to timeout and a day without screen time. I am a therapist, how I help them navigate through emotional storms and hold them until rainbows form. I used to answer the question by saying I'm "just a dad". Now I know I'm so much more.

There's no blueprint or manual. Every role is tailor made to fit the temperament and needs of each child. The epitome of on the job training. Parenthood is something that none of us really had the credentials for but were qualified by our scars. Even when I don't feel up to par I'm verified. Terrified of failure but I raise the bar and work hard. Cause this role gives me purpose. Helps me live deeper than the surface. This hard work is worth it. My past jobs weren't worthless. No experience was wasted. It was just preparation.

Although I can't brag about a high paying vocation this occupation is literally healing generations. Paying me with dividends of eternal memories. With benefits of priceless lessons about patience and empathy. My daughter's teaching me to be sensitive. And even though it's frustrating only being able to work part-time jobs for now. Although it's the hardest thing I've had to do. And although my role doesn't fit society's demands of me as a man. I can honestly say I'm proud to be a stay-at-home dad.

Masks

Today is Halloween. We celebrate haunted houses, scaring people, and eating sweets we get from strangers. But besides the skeletons, monsters, ghosts, and spiders, in some sense, we're celebrating fakeness over authenticity. Because on this day, we're just doing what we do every other day externally. To say it simply, most of us put on masks, costumes, and facial facades as daily routines. We hide our insecurities-- with smiles, we shove down our pain-- with fake laughs, and overcompensate for things we think we lack with masks.

Throwing our mirrors, and identities in the trash cause we were tired of looking at ugliness. And yes it's ironic, on Halloween we wear masks to scare people away and make 'em afraid. But any other day we're scared of what others may think and say if they saw our true faces, so we wear masks because we're afraid. Afraid that I can't handle the hidden pain and inner shame. Afraid that when the mask comes off I'll see a monster.

Afraid that you'll see my scars that I got from trauma. Afraid that I'm not beautiful underneath. Afraid that I wore this mask for so long I can't remember the real me. Hiding skeletons in our closets have turned our hearts to Haunted Houses. Our comfort amens as the church allows this.

It's time to carve through our denial so we can shine our lights through like Jack-O-Lanterns. Because we were created unique and diverse, for love and self-worth, the first sin brought this curse, but since death has been swerved. You can leave your masks 6 feet under the dirt. Because I hear God knocking on the door to your heart like Trick-or-Treat on October 31st.

Saying "Let me take your mask. Let me in because I see what you don't see. You see weakness. I see beauty underneath. There's a reflection of me in you that the world needs to see. There's healing that needs to sink deep. But I won't force you so please." You see, these masks are nothing but protection. External projections instead of true expression. Hiding under the shadow of rejection. Isolation is the perpetrator of depression.

These masks keep others out but locks the hurt inside. And you're worth being seen. You shouldn't have to become someone else for love. Because who you are now is enough. I know it's rough. Unmasking will be tough. You will have to deal with some hidden stuff. But if you're fed up with all the bluffs it's time to stand up. Enough is enough. Your silence is crying out for hope. So you can put your smile aside and cry for once. Your heart is dying to live. So yeah you might put on a costume tonight but don't let it consume you tomorrow. Many of us have masks on, I'm afraid of unmasking too. But will you take it off and let us see the real you?

Power and Disappointment

I'm caught in the middle. Tension building like unsolved riddles. Belief brittle. Used to have sky-high zeal now my faith feels so little. Cause well.. she died of cancer, leaving questions unanswered. After years of prayer all that's left is .. frustration, failed expectations, and self-condemnation. Cause they said my lack of faith can hinder manifestations. God why didn't you heal her? You are the healer. Broken bones, heart murmurs, and hernias bow down in your presence. Powerful and mighty. So why does it seem like your hands were tied behind when she cried out in pain, did you turn a blind eye? How am I supposed to believe in situations like these? But how can I not after everything I've seen. I mean, she was like a second mother to me. Many times we laid hands and prayed, as your power flowed through her veins, ailments healed in Jesus name. Yet the same hands that were anointed grew cold, leaving my grieving soul disappointed. God, your Kingdom manifest through her very own body yet her flesh fell victim to cancer cells harshly. Breaking her down. How do I live in the now? While we expect for a Kingdom already but not yet. There's not enough anointing oil that can raise her from the soil, in my timing. So how do I wait for yours? While the clocks ticking and my just grandpa passed away from COVID's affliction. How can strength be made perfect in weakness? When bitterness seeks to reach in, stealing joy like leeches, darkness trying to block out the Son's light like a solar eclipse. Jesus I'm sad, mad, and I guess I just don't understand. Sometimes things don't happen according to our demands.

———

Abandonment

I wish I could handle abandonment like a magic trick. Pull healing out of a hat, then bam— watch it vanish. Instead I'm tryna manage this emotional hypnosis, but I can't snap out of it. These damages go unnoticed because I just throw on a couple bandages and become a savage so it won't happen again.

I know every relationship has its challenges but trusting feels like gambling so I'm not down to risk. They say I'm safe now but the past shows I haven't been. Battling circumstances with a heart full of calluses. I'm skeptical. In every relationship from platonic to sexual I would rather die than become someone susceptible. My pride on the pedestal. Trauma's a bitch and my body knows her chemicals. So now I leave you before you leave me, and act like I'm glad you're gone.

But when I'm on my own I listen to sad songs and realize wrongs. Even though I abandoned I'm the one mad at y'all. This pattern runs my life like a marathon. Isolation is my drug of choice and I am far far gone. I learned early on that connection is a revolving door. The real question is how long are you here for? If you're anything like my flings, ex's, and friendships you'll leave for sure.

I set standards low so alone is the norm. Walls up waiting to be torn down. Heart cold from this war. I'm worn out. I fight with a double-edged sword 'cause the world taught me how. Self-sabotage smiles into frowns while the power of control keeps my head in the clouds. Until it all crashes down into the ground.

Cause I've had partners leave me for my best friends. Everywhere around I'm still seeing this trend. Codependent souls trying to make amends. And I remember how my best friends fled when I stopped doing drugs. Maybe they were so sick of me they were looking for an excuse to pull the plug. And it may be selfish to say but why do i feel like my wife's suicide was her attempt to get away… from me.

These were all different chapters but I'm the one constant factor so maybe I'm the cancer after all. I mean my pastors even switched up so do you expect me to trust god? So maybe I'm flawed. Maybe it's my fault? Or maybe just caught in a spin doing what I've been taught?

———

I Am by Tiala Balane

I am sick and optimistic

I wonder if anyone will finally love me, and all of me

I hear a constant tick

I see the tick on my life clock, ticking so fast in front of me

I want my life clock to slow down,

I know the ticks are just seconds of the minutes, the minutes of the hours, and the hours of my day

I am sick and optimistic

I pretend to be happy, sometimes I actually am.

It depends on the tick of my life clock or the minute, hour, or day.

I feel like an engineer trying to reverse the time on a watch,

So I have more time or even take back the time I've wasted

I touch my pulse to make sure I'm still alive

I worry that I won't be able to make up for my mistakes, and I won't live to thrive

I cry when I see myself in the mirror—

A couple of years older, I see my inner child in my reflection

I am sick and optimistic

I understand that I am not the broken child,

Nor anywhere near who I was in my dark hole of addiction.

That's something I want to mention.

I say I am Tiala Balane— a mother and wife.

I dream of the day I can look back at my one life through a new set of eyes.

I try to live my life sober and with no more lies.

reviews

Enjoy this book? You can make a big difference!

Reviews are the most powerful tool when it comes to getting atten-tion for writing a book. Not only would I love to read your kind words, I'd really like to hear your honest feedback.

If you've enjoyed reading or learning from this book, please consider telling your friends about it or take five minutes to write a review on the book's Amazon page.

Thank you,

Matt

about the author

Matt Balane is a conscious hip-hop artist, spoken word poet, and inspirational speaker based from the Inland Empire area. Known for his raw honesty and powerful storytelling, Matt brings a message of resilience and healing to audiences worldwide. His work, which focuses on mental health, identity, and hope, resonates with youth, people in recovery, and anyone navigating life's challenges.